DIGITAL AND INFORMATION LITERACY™

BIT ROT
PRESERVING THE DOCUMENTS MOST IMPORTANT TO YOU

MARCIA AMIDON LUSTED

rosen publishing's
rosen central®

New York

Published in 2017 by The Rosen Publishing Group, Inc.
29 East 21st Street, New York, NY 10010

Library of Congress Cataloging-in-Publication Data

Names: Lusted, Marcia Amidon, author.
Title: Bit rot : preserving the documents most important to you / Marcia Amidon Lusted.
Description: New York : Rosen Publishing, 2017. | Series: Digital and information literacy | Audience: Grade 5-8. | Includes bibliographical references and index.
Identifiers: LCCN 2016017409| ISBN 9781499465174 (library bound) | ISBN 9781499465150 (pbk.) | ISBN 9781499465167 (6-pack)
Subjects: LCSH: Digital preservation–Juvenile literature.
Classification: LCC Z701.3.C65 L87 2017 | DDC 025.8/4–dc23
LC record available at https://lccn.loc.gov/2016017409

Manufactured in China

CONTENTS

	Introduction	4
Chapter 1	Here Today, Gone Tomorrow	7
Chapter 2	A Picture's Worth a Thousand Bytes	14
Chapter 3	From Paper Trail to No Trail	21
Chapter 4	Music in the Air…and Nowhere Else	28
Chapter 5	Preserving the Future	34
	Glossary	40
	For More Information	41
	For Further Reading	44
	Bibliography	45
	Index	47

INTRODUCTION

Has this ever happened to you? You've spent hours writing a paper or putting together a special presentation on your computer for school. You think you've saved it, but then something happens. Your file is gone, vanished without a trace, and you don't know why. Now you have to reconstruct the project before it's due…tomorrow.

And do you remember all those photos that you took of your friends when you all went to the beach last summer? Maybe they are still on your phone, or maybe you have them on a memory card or on your computer. You've never quite gotten around to printing them out, but you'll do it sometime. After all, they aren't going anywhere, right?

Most people in the digital age are accustomed to thinking that their computer files and other digital information is safe and that it will always be accessible when they want it. This not only includes documents and photographs, but also all those MP3 files for downloaded music, as well as movies and e-books. They may have cost hundreds of dollars to download, so most people feel like they "own" them for as long as they want them. But, unlike a physical paper book, a CD of music, or an album of photographs, digital files have an uncertain lifespan. Perhaps we get new computers and either don't or can't transfer the old files to them. Or the platform used for

Using tablets and other digital platforms has become common both for fun and for work and school.

those files becomes obsolete and there's no way to open them anymore (think about all those videotapes of movies your family might still have and how impossible they are to watch since your old videocassette recorder broke). Computer files are useless if the technology to read them no longer exists. Or a computer may crash, or a smartphone may fall into the water, and suddenly the files on those machines are corrupted or have simply disappeared.

Losing digital files and data isn't simply a matter of inconvenience. It can also affect how companies and organizations function. It can even affect history. The National Aeronautics and Space Administration (NASA) has already lost data from some of the first missions to the moon because that data was encoded on tapes and the machines needed to read those tapes have long since been turned into scrap and cannot be rebuilt. Technology is advancing so quickly that a digital storage method that is popular and widespread today might be totally obsolete in a few years, just as movies on videotape gave way to DVDs and Blu-ray, which in turn are being replaced with digital downloads.

It is very important to understand not only why digital files are not a safe and permanent means of storing data and important information, but also how both large companies, organizations, governments, and libraries, as well as the average person, can safeguard their digital files to make sure that they can continue to be accessed for years and even decades.

Chapter 1

Here Today, Gone Tomorrow

Not that long ago, within your grandparents' and even your parents' lifetimes, almost everything was saved as a hard copy. Important documents like certificates, insurance policies, historical archives, and public records were all filed as paper copies. This required a lot of filing space and a lot of work. In some cases, a fire at a public courthouse or a town hall could completely destroy documents, leaving behind no records of vital information.

For many offices, the days of paper and file folders taking up huge amounts of space are over, thanks to digital records.

File   Edit   View   Favorites   Tools   Help

ANCIENT DATA LOSS

Ancient Data Loss

One of the most famous losses of information happened long before the Information Age…in fact, it happened more than two thousand years ago! The Ancient Library of Alexandria in Egypt held half a million paper scrolls and books that contained all the important mathematical, scientific, and literary works of the entire world. Most of the scrolls and books were the only ones in existence—one of a kind with no backup copies. When the library was burned during the Siege of Alexandria in 48 BC, all of its archives were destroyed. It is still considered to be the greatest symbol of knowledge and culture being destroyed.

It's a Digital World

Today we live in the digital age. Things that used to be saved on paper are now saved electronically on computers, in digital form. In some ways, this is better. Fewer trees are chopped down to make paper for documents, files are easily accessed without having to sort through file cabinets, and people all over the world can access each other's records and documents with just a few keystrokes, instead of requesting documents that have to be copied and mailed. Banking and bill paying are easily done online, without mailing paper copies back and forth.

However, there are drawbacks to digital records. According to Abraxas, a digital records management company, "There are many advantages to electronic record keeping. Typically, it allows for easier storage, accessibility and backup of vital records, all at lower cost. But there are disadvantages as well. Virtual files may require special equipment in order to read them. Hardware and software changes may render older files inaccessible. Some organizations may not manage electronic records as diligently as they do paper files."

A Nasty Disease?

But perhaps the biggest threat to anything that is created or saved digitally is something known as bit rot. It sounds like a nasty disease, and for digital data, it is. Bit rot, which is also known by the names bit decay, data rot, data decay, and silent corruption, is the slow deterioration in the performance and integrity of data stored on storage media. It means that over time, the magnetic qualities of digital and computer files will degrade. It might not even be noticeable or might seem like a small glitch in a file. As technology site Ars Technica describes it:

> One at a time, year by year, a random bit [short for binary digit, the smallest unit of data in a computer] here or there gets flipped. If you have a malfunctioning drive or controller—or a loose/faulty cable—a lot of bits might get flipped. Bitrot is a real thing, and it affects you more

Bit rot can turn a JPEG photograph into a series of strange rainbow stripes, making it impossible to see the original image.

than you probably realize. The JPEG that ended in blocky weirdness halfway down? Bitrot. The MP3 that startled you with a violent CHIRP!, and you wondered if it had always done that? No, it probably hadn't—blame bitrot. The video with a bright green block in one corner followed by several seconds of weird rainbowy blocky stuff before it cleared up again? Bitrot.

The problem of bit rot also includes files becoming obsolete when the medium or technology they are saved on is no longer generally used or available, like those old eight-track and cassette music tapes your grand-parents have or a ten-year-old video game that no one has a gaming console for anymore.

Cassette tapes, which could be played on a portable device like this Walkman, are now a nearly obsolete technology.

Just Passing Through

Content on the internet is not safe from bit rot, either. Websites come and go, and their content becomes unavailable if that company goes out of business. Much of daily life today is captured digitally online, in tweets, emails, and on Facebook, to name just a few. Even cloud storage companies, which allow customers to store their valuable data files online in a way that can be accessed from anywhere, often go out of business. According to one research firm quoted in *Computer World* magazine, one in four cloud providers had been forced out of business between 2013 and 2015, mostly through company mergers. Sometimes clients had time to retrieve their data before those clouds went away, but sometimes they did not.

Digital data is also vulnerable to other factors. A power loss or power surge can fry a computer and wipe out its files. An electromagnetic pulse (EMP) from a nuclear bomb could destroy huge amounts of data. Files can be corrupted or destroyed by cyberterrorism, viruses, and even extreme heat, cold, or dampness. Some data is stored or run on proprietary software (also called closed-format files), which is software that belongs to a particular company, organization, or individual and can be used only if the user purchases a license from that company. In contrast, open-format files can be accessed for free by anyone.

So Many Ways to Get Lost

There are, in short, many ways that data files can be lost. They can be corrupted, their media becomes obsolete, they can be lost when a company goes out of business and takes the files with them, or they might be destroyed by a power surge. What happens as a result of losing files? Personal documents and family photographs are lost or inaccessible. Businesses lose records, invoices, and employee files. Governments lose vital records. Historical documents, including visual and audio files of historic events, are gone. Media like movies, historical television and radio broadcasts of historic events, and television shows disappear. Much of our personal and collective documents and cultural artifacts no longer exist.

Today, many different kinds of files are saved digitally. Each type of file is vulnerable in its own way and requires its own safeguards and precautions. And some of the most common and most vulnerable types of files are those that we all have: photographs.

TEN GREAT QUESTIONS
TO ASK A DIGITAL PRESERVATIONIST

1 Is it hopeless to try to preserve digital files for the future?

2 How can you make sure that a digital file always stays the same when it is archived?

3 Does it cost a lot of money to preserve digital files?

4 Should we worry about a time in the future when there might not be computers or technology?

5 Which files are worth saving and which aren't?

6 Why should we worry about saving digital files?

7 Once I back up my digital files, are they good forever?

8 If I accidentally lose my files, is there a way to get them back?

9 Is it better to use a cloud system, an online database, or a hard drive for backing up files?

10 Can old film movies be saved as digital files?

Chapter 2

A Picture's Worth a Thousand Bytes

Not that long ago, photographs were taken using film. Photographers took many photos of the same subject because they could not see if an image had come out right at the time of the photo. Once a roll of film was finished, it was taken to a developer or developed in a home darkroom. The end result was a set of printed photos, which could then be saved in an album or framed, or even just saved in a box or folder. The film itself, with its series of images (called negatives), was also saved, and the negatives could be used to make additional copies of an image.

What's Film?

Today it can be hard even to find film for film cameras. Photography, like so many other things, has gone digital. Not only do we take photos with digital cameras, and see how they came out seconds after we took them, but we can use our phones, tablets, and computers to take photos as well. Those photos are stored on devices, as computer files, or on a memory stick

With film cameras, images were made into negatives, which were then developed into photographs in a darkroom.

or memory card. They can still be printed out for framing or sharing, but more commonly we share photos on social media or by emailing them to each other. There are even frames that display a changing slideshow of photographs without needing to print them out at all. Many people prefer digital photographs to hard copies mounted in traditional photo albums, especially younger people who are used to scrolling through slideshows on a computer or phone. Instead of inheriting a huge cardboard box full of family photos, they would prefer to inherit a hard drive filled with those same photos.

Photographs that exist as digital files on a computer or other device are safer than printed copies when it comes to damage from things like fire, water, or even just wear and tear. However, digital files are vulnerable in different ways. They can be accidentally deleted or overwritten. If they are

A Digital Dark Age?

Vint Cerf, a vice president of Google, worries that the twenty-first century could become a digital dark age, just like the Dark Ages in history when there were few records kept and historians don't know very much about what life was like. "We stand to lose a lot of our history. If you think about the quantity of documentation from our daily lives which is captured in digital form, like our interactions by email, people's tweets, all of the world wide web, then if you wanted to see what was on the web in 1994 you'd have trouble doing that. A lot of the stuff disappears. We don't want our digital lives to fade away. If we want to preserve them the same way we preserve books and so on we need to make sure that the digital objects we create will be rendered far into the future."

stored on a device like a phone or tablet, those devices can be lost or damaged and the photos will also be lost. And as with any digital files, they are only as good as the software used to open them. If people twenty years in the future try to open files with a generation of family photographs, they may not be able to if the software used to save them is now obsolete.

Lose Your Phone, Lose Your Photos

Storing photos on a phone is not a good option, either. "Photos are some of the most important files you'll ever create. We're taking more photos than ever—an estimated 900 billion photos will be uploaded to the web this year. And billions more live on our camera rolls, waiting for us to back them up, erase them, or—amazingly—simply discard them when we give up and buy a new phone," said Casey Newton of the website The Verge.

Another danger with digital-only photography is that photographers may delete images that seem unimportant at the time but might have historic significance later. Perhaps they delete an image of someone who later becomes very famous. According to Vint Cerf, "Historians will tell you that sometimes documents, transactions, images and so on may turn out to have an importance which is not understood for hundreds of years. So failure to preserve them will cause us to lose our perspective."

What Can You Do?

So what can be done to make sure that the photos we take today can still be enjoyed years in the future? The simplest thing to do is to print them out. As Vint Cerf says:

We have various formats for digital photographs and movies and those formats need software to correctly render those objects. Sometimes the standards we use to produce those objects fade away and are replaced by other alternatives and

Today, many department stores and drugstores have machines that customers can easily use themselves to edit and print out their digital photographs.

then software that is supposed to render images can't render older formats, so the images are no longer visible. If there are pictures that you really really care about then creating a physical instance is probably a good idea. Print them out, literally.

Another way to make sure that photos stay safe is to make a second copy of them on an SD memory card or memory stick. Then give the stick to a friend or a family member who doesn't live in the same house. That way, if the stick is lost or there is a fire or other disaster in the house, there will still

Saving digital photographs on a memory stick is a good way to back up those same files that are on your computer.

be a backup copy of the photo files somewhere else. It is also important to use features like write protection on an SD card to prevent someone from accidentally writing over the files on it.

There are also cloud services for storing photos. Companies like Amazon, Apple, and Google offer cloud storage for photos, and there are also dedicated websites that provide the same service. It is important to find a reputable service that won't suddenly go out of business, losing its customers' photos, and it's still a good idea to have a second type of backup, such as an SD card.

Gone...but Maybe Not Forever

If the worst happens and photos are accidentally deleted from a memory stick, SD card, or hard drive, there are services that specialize in data recovery and can often recover lost photo files. There are also software programs available that can be used to find deleted files, instead of using a recovery service.

Safeguarding photographs by backing them up or printing them out can be time-consuming. But if it's done regularly, it isn't difficult. Many photographs are priceless memories of family, friends, and special events, and it's well worth the extra time and effort to keep them safe and accessible.

Chapter 3

From Paper Trail to No Trail

Paper is one of the most ancient technologies for saving important documents, letters, and books. Since its invention in ancient China, paper made from wood pulp has been easy to make and affordable in cost. As a result, it changed society because documents and books could be produced easily and made accessible to everyone.

Paper Is Not Perfect

However, paper is one of the most fragile materials for saving valuable documents. It is vulnerable to dampness, can be easily ripped, and burns quickly. Many historic archives of records and letters have been destroyed by fires in places like libraries and courthouses or by natural disasters, such as flooding. Paper files also take up a great deal of space in file cabinets and other storage systems.

The advent of computers and digital files made it possible to take a whole building filled with file cabinets of documents and store them instead

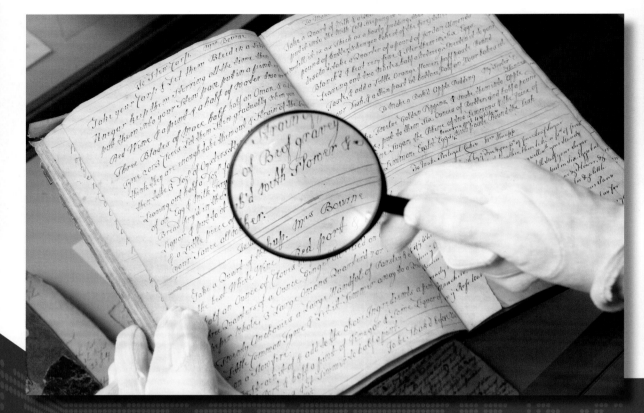

Old books and documents are extremely fragile, so making digital copies of them is a good way to ensure that they will be easy to access and the originals will last.

as digital files on one computer. They are much more easily accessed, too. People can find files without physically having to go to where they are located. They can simply use their computers to access those files digitally. Many museums and historical societies have scanned their historic documents into digital versions that users can access from anywhere in the world. This has two advantages: people can do research remotely, and the fragile original documents, letters, and books aren't further damaged by too much handling. It also keeps the original documents safely in climate-controlled environments that will preserve them.

File   Edit   View   Favorites   Tools   Help

PRINT IS NOT DEAD

Print Is Not Dead

When e-books became popular, many people feared that print books would become obsolete. Booksellers worried about their business as people bought more e-books and print book sales went down. But as of 2015, according to *The New York Times*, print book sales have risen again and many e-book companies are struggling. Most readers, however, seem to like a combination of technologies. They might read e-books while traveling but read print books at home.

Paper or Digital?

Books, too, have benefitted from the creation of e-books, which are read on a tablet, phone, or computer. E-books can be a huge space saver since physical books take up a great deal of space in homes and offices. They make entire libraries easily available no matter where a reader might be, they are easier to carry when traveling, and like digital documents, they save paper and trees. Many e-books can be borrowed from libraries or obtained for free. And e-books aren't subject to the same damage that paper books are.

However, digital documents and e-books are vulnerable to the same technological hazards as photographs. Many document files are written in proprietary software, such as Microsoft Word. This means that Microsoft owns the technology used to create those documents, and anyone who wants to access them has to have a license for Word, which costs money. To make things even more difficult, older documents may not be accessible in newer versions of the software.

Many people prefer to read e-books on tablets or e-readers, but if those devices fail or become out of date, the copies of the books they hold will be lost.

E-books can suffer from similar problems. It's even more complicated because there are many different software platforms for e-books, such as Kindle, Nook, Microsoft Ereader, and many others. E-books that are purchased and downloaded for an iPad can't usually be read on a Kindle. In addition, reading devices can become obsolete so that they are no longer useable. If the user doesn't update the software on the device, or if it simply becomes too old, it loses the ability to download new books or even to work at all. If someone owns a whole library of books on an e-reader or computer and that device crashes or no longer works, then their entire library is gone.

Hard Copies and Soft Copies

So what can be done to make sure that important documents, letters, records, and books are not lost if their software becomes obsolete or the device they were intended for is no longer available? The simplest method is, just as with photographs, to print out documents or buy hard copies of books. For paper items that are irreplaceable or extremely important, this is probably still the best way to make sure that they are always accessible.

For documents that are created in a word-processing program, one way to make sure that they will be readable for as long as possible is to save them as a PDF (Portable Document Format) or PDF/A (the extra *A* stands for "Archival"). PDFs were created to capture documents and any text, fonts,

A combination of hard paper copies and digital copies is the best way to make sure that important documents won't be lost forever.

images, and formatting they contain and have them look the same, no matter what platform they are being read on. That means you can save a school paper with photos on it as a PDF using your PC computer, email it to your teacher who uses a Mac computer, and have it look exactly the same on the teacher's screen as it does on yours.

Looking Long-Term

Long-term solutions are needed so that many of the documents and records that are important to history won't be lost when their technology is obsolete. According to Vint Cerf of Google:

> **Another potential solution is developing "digital vellum" [vellum is parchment made from calfskin, and is durable and long-lasting] to preserve software, hardware and all of today's technology programs so that files can be saved and preserved for generations. An X-ray snapshot of the content and the application and the operating system together, with a description of the machine that it runs on, [can] preserve that for long periods of time.**

It is also a good idea to save important documents on an external hard drive or to a cloud system, so that there is a backup copy of anything that's really irreplaceable for family history or household records. Cloud storage should be done through a company that is established and unlikely to go out of business, such as Microsoft or Amazon. An extra layer of protection would be to save vital documents on a memory stick or another hard drive and have a friend or a family member in a different household keep them. As with any digital file, the more ways that your documents can be backed up and saved, the better the chances of accessing them in the future.

MYTHS & FACTS

MYTH Free software and online tools will always be free and accessible.

FACT The free software that is used to open and run a program or file today may not be free, or even accessible, in the future.

MYTH The internet is the only digital library most people need.

FACT Using the internet can be a very difficult way to get information. Finding it is difficult, the quality varies widely, and there are few resources to help people find the right information.

MYTH Digital libraries provide more equal access to books, anywhere and at any time.

FACT For most of the world, internet access is not easy or even available at all. Computers may also need special hardware and software to access books digitally.

Chapter 4

Music in the Air... and Nowhere Else

More than anything else, the way that we save and access music and movies has changed rapidly. It's hard to imagine that people once listened to music only on vinyl records, eight-track and cassette tapes, and CDs. All of these formats were vulnerable. Records warped or developed scratches that made the music skip or repeat. Tapes stretched or broke and had a limited lifespan, especially if they were left in extreme hot or cold conditions. CDs could also become scratched. With the invention of MP3 files for music, downloading and listening to music became much simpler and faster and could be done without a trip to the store to buy hard copies of albums and songs. Many musicians are also now releasing their music only in digital format, with no hard copy versions available at all.

Back in the Old Days...

It's also hard to remember that not that long ago, most people could watch movies only at the movie theater or on television. Then the videocassette

Music stores used to provide listening stations where customers could hear a CD before they purchased it.

recorder (VCR) was invented, and movies could be watched in Beta and VHS formats. Beta disappeared, and eventually VHS videos were replaced by DVDs and Blu-ray. Even these are beginning to reach obsolescence as more and more people stream their movies from the internet. As for family videos, they were originally recorded on movie film such as Super 8, which

The Super 8 movie camera was the first system available for regular people to make home movies simply and cheaply.

was a type of movie film, cameras, and projectors that debuted in 1965. Super 8 made it possible for average people to make movies easily and inexpensively. Then, with the invention of the VCR, home videos could be taken using videocassettes. Today we use our phones to take videos digitally and share them instantly.

Can You Hear Me Now?

All of these new technologies have made accessing music and movies instantaneous. But they are also vulnerable, just like other digital forms of information. An MP3 is a compressed file that saves music in a digital form that is much smaller than the original but still sounds like the original when played. It is extremely popular for storing music on portable devices, such as iPods and MP3 players.

But MP3 files can suffer from bit rot over time, making the music skip or stop when it is played. Even good MP3 files might not be transferrable between devices, depending on the program used to listen to that music. An example is the Apple iTunes application, which allows only limited sharing from one device to another. MP3 files are also just as vulnerable as any digital file to being lost or corrupted or simply stuck on an obsolete device. Unless users create backup files on other devices, they may lose all of their music library. According to the Technology Guide website:

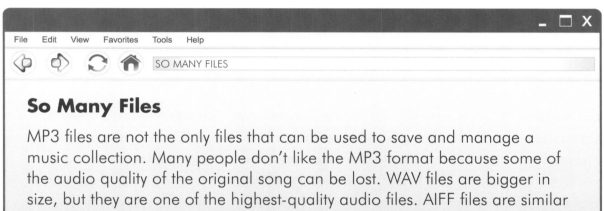

So Many Files

MP3 files are not the only files that can be used to save and manage a music collection. Many people don't like the MP3 format because some of the audio quality of the original song can be lost. WAV files are bigger in size, but they are one of the highest-quality audio files. AIFF files are similar to WAV, but they were created by Apple and are not as widely used. FLAC files fall between MP3 and WAV files because they have better sound quality than MP3s but aren't quite as big as WAV files. However, most media players don't support FLAC files, and devices need to have special software downloaded in order to make them play. WMA (Windows Audio Media) is a good-quality type of music file, but only for people who are only going to listen to their music on a computer that runs Windows software.

If you have music files stored on your hard drive but have never taken steps to back those files up, you're playing a dangerous game. At any moment, a wayward power surge or freak drive malfunction could render your entire music collection kaput. Considering the average album costs about $10 to download, you could easily be looking at thousands of dollars in losses.

Backing It Up

The best way to make sure that music files will be accessible in case of a system or device failure is to back them up. They can be burned onto a DVD or CD, if a computer still has that technology, stored on a memory stick or external hard drive, stored on a smartphone or MP3 player, or stored on a cloud system. iCloud, Amazon, Google, and Dropbox are all good cloud systems from reputable companies that aren't likely to suddenly go out of business, taking your entire music library with them. Some people argue for still buying albums on CD (and vinyl records are also making a comeback) so that listeners have them as a hard copy that they actually own, and not just as a digital file. But again, those files are only as good as the devices they need to play them. In coming years, record players and CD players may be difficult or impossible to find and use.

Movies can be even more difficult to store over time. Movie technology has changed so rapidly that many families still have movies on video, DVD, and Blu-ray, along with the players needed for each format, as well as subscriptions to online streaming services such as Netflix or Amazon. For old family movies on film or video, the only way to ensure that they will still be available is to make them into AVI (for PC or Mac computers) or MOV (for Mac computers) files that can be digitally stored on a hard drive, or at least to transfer them to DVD format. AVI and MOV files are large, uncompressed formats that aren't recommended for easy playback or sharing because they are so large. However, they are the most durable and lasting file formats

Devices like iPhones can easily store digital music files, but they should still be backed up to cloud storage or a computer.

and the most likely to be compatible with future technologies. There is also the MPEG4 file format, which makes compressed files that can be easily shared on the internet or by email, and can be played on mobile devices, like smartphones.

When it comes to music and movies, digital technology has made saving these files easier than ever. But since they don't often exist as tangible objects, such as a CD or a DVD, they are also vulnerable to loss. For people who don't want shelves full of DVDs or a stack of music CDs, it's important to back up movie and music libraries in several places, so that a favorite song or much-loved movie will always be there when they want it.

Chapter 5

Preserving the Future

I t may seem like bit rot is a disease without a real cure when it comes to saving important digital files like photographs, documents, music, and movies. But there are things that can be done to make sure that these things are saved for posterity.

What's the Password?

Governments and libraries have been developing ways to save many digital items, although it can be difficult to archive websites and programs that are privately owned by a company and not accessible without a password or other credential. The Library of Congress has a digital preservation program that it began in 2000. It tries to archive websites that are part of America's cultural heritage. It has about ten thousand websites archived now, but permission to archive many sites is hard to get.

The Internet Archive is a private nonprofit company that hosts the Wayback Machine, a popular internet service that lets users see what a web page looked like on a certain date. It also includes other digital media such

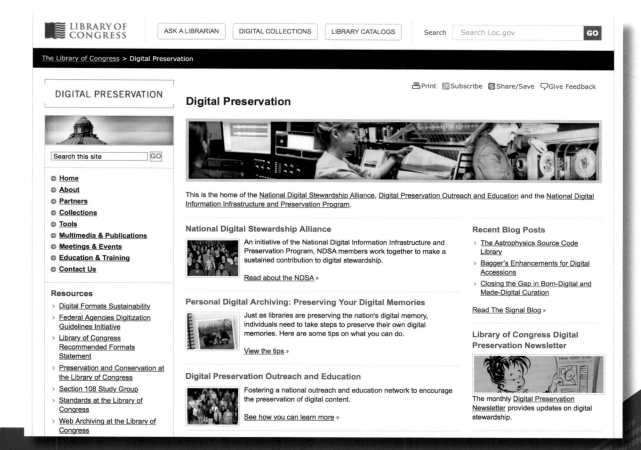

The Library of Congress website has many resources about digital preservation. Saving digital files has long been a priority of this organization.

as books, software, and videos. It has presently archived about 160 billion websites, according to *The Economist*. But to archive everything of importance successfully, archivists have to worry about permissions and copyrights. "To do this properly, the rights of preservation might need to be incorporated into our thinking about things like copyright and patents and licensing. "We're talking about preserving them for hundreds to thousands of years," said Vint Cerf of Google.

Rot and RAID

There are some other ways to capture both digital files and the software needed to run them. According to an article in *The Guardian*:

> Researchers at Carnegie Mellon University in Pittsburgh have made headway towards a solution to bit rot, or at least a partial one. There, [they take] digital snapshots of computer hard drives while they run different software programs. These can then be uploaded to a computer that mimics the one the software ran on. The result is a computer that can read otherwise defunct files.

Another possible solution for preservation is RAID technology. "RAID" stands for "Redundant Array of Independent Disks," and it is basically a system in which a large number of inexpensive hard drives are combined into one high-capacity storage drive. It can be used to back up large amounts of data safely. It is also important that software makers adopt open-format standards, meaning that their software is free to use. This means that any digital files created in that software can be saved and viewed later without the need for permission or special access to that software.

Back Up, Back Up, Back Up

But what can average people do to preserve their own important papers, files, and family histories? The easy answer is to back up, back up, back up! Print out documents and photos and keep them in a safe place. Then back up those digital files to hard drives, memory sticks, and clouds and keep backup media in different places so that a fire or natural disaster doesn't destroy all the hard and soft copies at once. And shift all files to a new, updated software or platform every five years, to make sure that your digital files don't get "trapped" in obsolete software or devices.

Another thing to consider is quality control when it comes to what is being saved. One of the advantages of digital publishing and digital music sharing is

Backing up files on an external hard drive is one way to make sure they aren't lost, but they should be backed up regularly.

that almost anyone can produce a digital book or MP3 of a song. But since these files aren't produced by a professional publisher or music studio, their quality can be questionable. Make sure that the files you're saving, and will continue to maintain, are worth the constant effort of preserving.

Preserving information and memories is important, but it's just as important to get out of the digital world, have fun, and make new memories.

To Save or Not to Save? That Is the Question

The biggest question we need to ask ourselves is if some files are acceptable to lose. We live in a world where we are endlessly barraged by information, music, movies, books, photographs, videos, tweets, and Facebook posts. Do we save everything that comes into our lives, until we are trapped by our stuff and our own personal archives? It's important to remember that the best way to cherish memories is to remember them, and we should focus on the present moment.

Many people who have lost all of their possessions, including family documents and photos, in a fire or flood or other disaster, later find that they don't really miss those physical objects that much after all. Yes, we should back up and preserve the things that have meaning for us and our families using digital resources and the latest software and platforms, but we should remember what is truly valuable and keep those things in our memories.

GLOSSARY

archive A collection of historical documents or records that provide information about a group of people, a place, or an institution.

artifact An object of historical or cultural interest, usually created by a human.

bit Short for "binary digit," the smallest unit of data used in a computer.

bit rot The slow decay of data that is stored on digital media.

cloud A network of remote servers on the internet, used to store, manage, and process data.

console A device that is designed for playing video games.

corruption Errors in computer data when it is read, stored, or transmitted.

degrade To break down or decay.

deterioration The process of becoming progressively worse.

device A piece of equipment or a machine designed to serve a special purpose or perform a special function.

digital Data that is expressed as a series of 0s and 1s on a computer.

eight-track A magnetic tape cartridge used in the 1960s and 1970s for playing music.

EMP Short for "electromagnetic pulse," a burst of electromagnetic energy caused by a nuclear explosion in the atmosphere.

encode To convert computer information or instructions into a particular type of file or format.

format The way that information is stored on a computer.

glitch A small problem or fault, a temporary malfunction.

magnetic Using the qualities of a magnet to create patterns to store data.

obsolete Something that is no longer used or is out of date.

scroll A roll of parchment or paper used for writing or drawing on.

virtual Something that exists on a computer or through software but is not a physical object.

American Library Association
50 East Huron Street
Chicago, IL 60611
(800) 545-2433
Website: www.ala.org
The American Library Association is the professional organization for
    librarians in the United States. One if its main concerns is the
    preservation of archival material.

Association of Research Libraries
21 Dupont Circle NW #800
Washington, DC 20036
(202) 296-2296
Website: www.arl.org
The Association of Research Libraries (ARL) is a nonprofit organization of
    124 research libraries at comprehensive research institutions in the
    United States and Canada that share similar research missions,
    aspirations, and achievements.

Canadian Digital Preservation Initiative
Canadiana
440 Laurier Avenue West, Suite 200
Ottawa, ON K1R 7X6
Canada
(613) 235-2628
Website: www.canadiana.org
Canadiana.org is a coalition of memory institutions dedicated to providing
    broad access to Canada's documentary heritage.

Canadian Library Association
1150 Morrison Drive, Suite 400
Ottawa, ON K2H 8S9
Canada
(613) 232-9625
Website: www.cla.ca
The Canadian Library Association is a professional organization for
    librarians in Canada.

Library of Congress
101 Independence Avenue SE
Washington, DC 20540
(202) 707-5000
Website: www.loc.gov
The premier archive in the United States, the Library of Congress has
    spearheaded a digital preservation program.

National Digital Stewardship Alliance
NDSA c/o CLIR+DLF
1707 L Street NW, Suite 650
Washington, DC 20036
(202) 939-4750
Website: http://www.digitalpreservation.gov/ndsa/NDSAtoDLF.html
This initiative of the National Digital Information Infrastructure and
    Preservation Program of the Library of Congress is implementing a
    national strategy to collect, preserve, and make available significant
    digital content, especially information that is created in digital form
    only, for current and future generations.

Websites

Because of the changing nature of internet links, Rosen Publishing has developed an online list of websites related to the subject of this book. This site is updated regularly. Please use this link to access this list:

http://www.rosenlinks.com/DIL/Bit

FOR FURTHER READING

Baby Professor. *Great Big World of Computers—History and Evolution*. Newark, DE: Speedy Publishing, 2015.

Baldridge, Aimee. *Organize Your Digital Life: How to Store Your Photographs, Music, Videos, and Personal Documents in a Digital World*. Washington, DC: National Geographic, 2009.

Carroll, Evan, and John Romano. *Your Digital Afterlife: When Facebook, Flickr and Twitter Are Your Estate, What's Your Legacy?* San Francisco, CA: New Riders, 2010.

Duffy, Jill E. *Get Organized: How to Clean Up Your Messy Digital Life*. Seattle, WA: PC Magazine, 2013.

Hagen, Mike. *Thousands of Images, Now What: Painlessly Organize, Save, and Back Up Your Digital Photos*. Malden, MA: Wiley, 2012.

Hawkins, Donald T. *Personal Archiving: Preserving Our Digital Heritage*. Medford, NJ: Information Today, Inc., 2013.

Levenick, Denise May. *How to Archive Family Keepsakes: Learn How to Preserve Family Photos, Memorabilia and Genealogy Records*. Cincinnati, OH: Family Tree Books, 2013.

Levenick, Denise May. *How to Archive Family Photos: A Step-by-Step Guide to Organize and Share Your Photos Digitally*. Cincinnati, OH: Family Tree Books, 2015.

Miller, Michael. *The Ultimate Digital Music Guide: The Best Way to Store, Organize, and Play Digital Music*. Indianapolis, IN: Que Publishing, 2012.

Rabbat, Suzy. *Post It! Sharing Photos with Friends and Family*. North Mankato, MN: Cherry Lake Publishing, 2012.

Suen, Anastasia. *Downloading and Online Shopping Safety and Privacy*. New York, NY: Rosen Publishing, 2013.

White, Ron. *How Computers Work*. Indianapolis, IN: Que Publishing, 2014.

BIBLIOGRAPHY

Abraxas "Paper vs. Electronic Files." (http://abraxasworldwide.com/kd-item
/paper-vs-electronic-files).

Alter, Alexandra. "The Plot Twist: E-Book Sales Slip, and Print Is Far From
Dead." *The New York Times*, September 22, 2015 (http://www.nytimes
.com/2015/09/23/business/media/the-plot-twist-e-book-sales-slip
-and-print-is-far-from-dead.html?_r=0).

Bartleet, Larry. "Your Kindle Will Turn Into a Relic If You Don't Update It
Today." NME, March 21, 2016 (http://www.nme.com/blogs/nme-
blogs/your-kindle-will-turn-into-a-relic-if-you-dont-update-it-today?
utm_source=facebook&utm_medium=social).

The Economist. "Digital data: Bit Rot." *The Economist*, April 28, 2012
(http://www.economist.com/node/21553445).

The Economist. "History Flushed," *The Economist*, April 28, 2012 (http://
www.economist.com/node/21553410).

Font, Vince. "How To Manage iTunes, MP3s, and Other Digital Music."
Technology Guide, October 4, 2013 (http://www.technologyguide
.com/howto/how-to-manage-your-music).

Font, Vince. "What's the Best Way to Back Up iTunes and Your Other
Music?" Technology Guide, August 14, 2013 (http://www
.technologyguide.com/feature
/whats-the-best-way-to-back-up-your-music).

Fuhrig, Lynda Schmitz. "Word-processing files need love, too." "The Bigger
Picture," Smithsonian Institution Archives, December 31, 2015 (http://
siarchives.si.edu/blog/word-processing-preservation).

Klaus, Amanda. "Scanning and Access." Augusta Museum of History (http://
www.augustamuseum.org/scanningandaccess).

Knapton, Sarah. "Print out digital photos or risk losing them, Google boss
warns." *The Telegraph,* February 13, 2015 (http://www.telegraph
.co.uk/news/science/science-news/11410506/Print-out-digital-photos

-or-risk-losing-them-Google-boss-warns.html).

McCoy, Mary. "6 Notorious Cases of Data Loss All Hosting Providers Can Learn From." R1 Blog, June 17, 2015 (http://www.r1soft.com /blog/6-notorious-cases-of-data-loss-all-hosting-providers-can-learn -from).

Mottl, Judy. "Internet Pioneer Vint Cerf Warns Of 'Bit Rot' And 'Digital Dark Age' But Don't Panic Yet." Tech Times, February 16, 2016 (http://www .techtimes.com/articles/32897/20150216/internet-pioneer-vint-cerf -warns-of-bit-rot-and-digital-dark-age-but-dont-panic-yet.htm).

Newton, Casey. "All-Time Greatest Album." The Verge. (http://www.theverge .com/2015/4/29/8467289 /cloud-photo-storage-comparison-dropbox-icloud-flickr-onedrive-free).

Rouse, Margaret. "Bit Rot Definition." Tech Target. (http://searchstorage .techtarget.com/definition/bit-rot).

Sample, Ian. "Google boss warns of 'forgotten century' with email and photos at risk." *The Guardian*, February 13, 2015 (http://www .theguardian.com/technology/2015/feb/13 /google-boss-warns-forgotten-century-email-photos-vint-cerf).

Slater, Jim. "Bitrot and atomic COWs: Inside "next-gen" filesystems." Ars Technica, January 15, 2014 (http://arstechnica.com/information -technology/2014/01 /bitrot-and-atomic-cows-inside-next-gen-filesystems).

Thibodeau, Patrick. "One in four cloud providers will be gone by 2015." *Computer World*, December 11, 2013 (http://www.computerworld .com/article/2486691/cloud-computing/one-in-four-cloud-providers -will-be-gone-by-2015.html).

INDEX

A

Amazon, 19, 26, 32
Apple, 19, 31
archives
    historical, 7, 21
    of websites, 34–35

B

Blu-ray, 6, 29, 32

C

cassette tapes, 10, 28
CDs, 4, 28, 32, 33
cloud storage companies, 11, 12, 19, 26,
    32, 36
cold, 11, 28
computer, 4, 8, 11, 14, 16, 21–24, 26,
    32, 36
    files on, 5, 9, 14, 16

D

dampness, 11, 21
devices, 14, 17, 24, 25, 31, 332, 3, 36
DVD, 29, 32, 33

E

e-books, 4, 23, 24
eight-track, 10, 28
external hard drive, 26, 32

F

film, 14, 16–17, 29–30, 32

G

Google, 16, 19, 26, 31, 32, 35

L

libraries, 8, 24, 27, 31, 32, 34

M

memory card, 4, 14, 16, 18, 20, 26, 32,
    36
movies, 4–5, 6, 12, 17, 28–30, 32, 33,
    34, 38
MP3 files, 4, 10, 28, 31, 36–37
music, 4, 10, 28, 30–34, 36–38

P

paper, 4, 7, 8, 21–22, 25, 26, 36
    as opposed to digital, 23–24
phone, 4, 5, 14, 16–17, 23, 30, 32, 33
photographs, 4, 11, 12, 14, 16¬–20, 23,
    25, 26, 34, 36, 38, 39
power surge, 11, 32

R

records, 7, 25, 26

S

software, 9, 11, 17–18, 20, 24, 25, 26,
    34–36, 3923

W

websites, 11, 17, 19, 34, 35

About the Author

Marcia Amidon Lusted has written 130 books and more than 500 magazine articles for young readers. As an editor, she was involved with digitizing an entire library of print magazines but knows that the best thing to do is have both hard copies and digital copies of anything important. She lives in New Hampshire, where she regularly backs up all her important files.

Photo Credits